SURVIVING
SCARY C

OLUFUNKE OGUNMODEDE

WRITE FOR GOLD PUBLISHING

Mailbox: funkie50babe@yahoo.co.uk
Instagram: https://www.instagram.com/funkieiamceo
Facebook: https://www.facebook.com/olufunke.ogunmodede

Published by
Write for Gold Publishing, United Kingdom

Dedication

This book is dedicated to God, survivors and to many women still going through the Scary C journey.

Acknowledgement

First and foremost, I want to thank my Lord and Saviour Jesus Christ for my life, that I am alive to share my story and rekindle hope in women, words are not enough to express my gratitude.

Bless the Lord Oh my soul and all that is within me, bless His Holy name.

I would like to thank my entire family, all my siblings with their husbands, wives and children and my very own adopted big sisters in Christ; Enitan Idowu, Shade Arise, thanks for your support, love, prayers, encouragement, and your time. I love you all, I will forever treasure you guys in my heart. To Wande Showunmi my very own personal HR director, gentle giant, I want to thank you specifically for the love, the countless outings; you take me out to any place of my choice, and you just listen to me…very priceless. I am so grateful, and I love you dearly.

Special thanks also goes to my church members NCC Edmonton, Living waters coordinators for their prayers and my spiritual Parents Rev Tayo and Bimbo Arowojolu for their continual spiritual support and care and words of encouragement.

I also wish to thank my beloved Sister Stella Maris Oji, who sowed the seed of me writing a book and my Bestie Bolanle Anifalaje, my encourager who continues to place a demand on my untapped potential. Dr Deji Yusuf, my dedicated coach, proof-reader, and editor for stretching my mind, working tirelessly, great patience, believing in me and helping me get this book to a publishing standard.

Finally, I would like to appreciate my very own loving and caring Hubby Femi Onabote who took great care of me physically and spiritually during the trying times, seeking God's face on his knees tirelessly. I love you! And to my wonderful sons Olaoluwa, Oluwadotun and Oluwafeolami my men of virtue, you dealt with the situation in your own ways. Thanks for caring for me in your little ways. You guys are my rock and world.... I love you so much.

Contents

Dedication 3

Acknowledgement.. 4

Testimonials 8

Endorsement 14

Foreword 16

Introduction 18

CHAPTER ONE.. 22

The Defining Moment 22

CHAPTER TWO.. 27

Bumpy Road Lies AHEAD 27

CHAPTER THREE 33

Bracing the Storm... 33

CHAPTER FOUR 41

You are not an island... 41

CHAPTER FIVE 47

Your thought tank What are your thoughts so far, beautiful? 47

CHAPTER SIX 53

MY FAITH.. 53

CHAPTER SEVEN 59

Your lifestyle matters 59

CHAPTER EIGHT... 66

Financial Aspect 66

CHAPTER NINE 75

My Support Groups 75

CHAPTER TEN 81

How did I ever get here? 81

CHAPTER ELEVEN 88

A TRIBUTE TO MY MENTOR.. 94

Final words: 98

Testimonials

On a personal level, having had a breast cancer diagnosis, I appreciated the care taken to touch on the various aspects I found myself having to consider; physical health of course, emotional health, mindset, spiritual health, family life, finances, having a support system and self-image - all of which this book addresses and more.

I appreciated the small details, which are actually important details, such as breaking the news to family members, crying when you need to, loving and appreciating yourself, being at peace and being kind to yourself at the same time, not isolating those who love and are caring for you but also realising that they too need a break and a breather sometimes. I am a details person and reading the details of how Olufunke Ogunmode managed and overcame her journey gave me hope and felt more gentle than reading a very direct list of facts, which is usually more the style of medical literature.

Anyone who has had a cancer diagnosis will know that you suddenly are given a large amount of information in a short amount of time that you have to digest and make informed decisions based on. Reading this book made it feel less overwhelming.   • **R Osholiki**

There is no doubt that the word 'Cancer' evokes fear whenever it is mentioned. This is even more so when someone is diagnosed with the dreaded disease. In fact, the fear of Cancer is probably worse than the diagnosis itself. No wonder, Olufunke Ogunmodede in this book refers to it as the 'Scary C' word.

In today's world, the word 'Cancer' is almost considered a death sentence. There is a feeling of helplessness and a resignation to fate where cancer is concerned. Therefore, it is quite encouraging to see someone who has gone through it and survived.

Using humor and illustrations, Olufunke has managed to treat this difficult subject with much panache and ease. Her simple writing style is impressive and makes for a compelling read! Olufunke tells her story right from the very beginning to the end, taking us through a very touching and emotional journey. I was held spell bound from the beginning of the book till the end.

A diagnosis of cancer is difficult to cope with. It is normal to feel anxious, frightened, or panicky at times. Fortunately, Olufunke's testimony comes in handy with all the necessary information. She has covered every aspect of her journey: diagnosis, treatment, family, faith, finances and even up to support system. What a journey! It is extremely hard to imagine that this is what the ALWAYS smiling Olufunke went through at the time. But she is an overcomer! A survivor!! This story

9

should serve as an encouragement to everyone going through the dreaded disease; anyone who has just been diagnosed or to those whose loved ones may be affected. My advice is to get the book and read it.

I have been privileged to attend the same church with Olufunke and have known her for over ten years. Even I cannot claim to know what she went through. When I felt led to suggest to her that she could tell her story for the benefit of others, little did I know what a compelling read it would be nor the fact that she would even take me up on it. **But I should have known the type of person our Olufunke is! She is an extremely courageous woman; kind-hearted with a staunch belief in God and most importantly, with a fierce desire and determination to help others**. - StellaMaris Oji

I n this memoir, Olufunke shares the story of her breast cancer journey in a way that engages the reader from the first chapter through to the last. Facing it head on, she has termed cancer 'the Scary C', and in this way, acknowledges her own vulnerability while encouraging cancer patients to own their story. This story shows us that there is hope for survival when the disease is detected and treated early.

10

Receiving a breast cancer diagnosis and undergoing treatment is no small feat. In addition to the physical effects of treatment and side effects, this story expresses the overwhelming feeling of a lack of control and the impact on one's mental health.

She highlights the importance of support which can be in various forms as it made a remarkable difference throughout her journey and recognizes that an individual can choose the form of support that feels comfortable.

This book raises a crucial point on the untold stories of those who support cancer patients; their careers who may be family or friends. The ones who show up, clean up, and stay up with raised chins and warm embraces. Although we may never hear their own stories, Olufunke urges us to take a moment and appreciate them for their unwavering love and care.

She shares on the impact of her diagnosis, treatment, and recovery, on her several roles as mother, wife, sister, and early years practitioner, and succinctly unearths the lessons she has learned on the way while staying anchored to her faith.

In every story, there's a part or phrase that stays with the reader long after the final chapter is read and for me it is this one:

"I concluded that I am not defined by all these challenges or changes happening to my body. There is more to me and my entire life. I am beautiful."

This book is inspiring and would encourage anyone going through a difficult situation. **- Mercy Ofuya, PhD**

Wow! Where do I start? I have read many Autobiographies in my lifetime, but I must say, Funkie's 'Scary C Journey' narrative is one of the most transparent, vulnerable, explicit, yet simplified and honest version I have ever read. Funky laid everything down bare in such a way that even the most 'Layperson' would read it and understand the story she is trying to tell.

I found the book riveting, candid, inspiring, encouraging, moving, fascinating, memorable, and most of all informative, all rolled into one. As I read each page, I went through numerous emotions.

I smiled, cried, sighed, held my breath, and sat on the edge of my seat. This book captivated me so much that I could not put it down. I literally read it from the beginning to the end non-stop in exactly two hours and nine minutes! I started reading it at 01:00 a.m. and finished it at 03:09a.m. It was a great read!

As a cover of someone going through the Scary C journey, many things resonated with me in Olufunke's book. It prepared me for things yet to come but also gave me courage and hope. Being a woman of faith myself like Funky, I have been able to let my faith and constant prayers play a major role in the way I now handle things, especially my mindset.

I have never met anyone so close to home who has gone through 'the whole nine yards' of the Scary C journey and has come out of it able to testify of such a positive outcome. It is mind-blowing!!

Olufunke's testimony has challenged me to be positive in a situation where all seems negative.

I would personally suggest that anyone going through the 'Scary C' journey or is connected in any way to anyone in such a position, to read this book and get a copy or copies for others, as I am convinced it would be an eye-opener and a blessing to them as it has been to me!

• E F UK

Endorsement

My Review:

"No one should ever have to go through the Scary C..."

I agree completely with that quote from the book written by Pastor Olufunke Ogunmodede. Even agreeing with her is an understatement because you have to be in her shoes to really understand how strong she has been, and how grace and mercy have seen her through.

I could remember the day she came to break the news that broke our hearts in the church New Covenant Church Edmonton. The devil implanted in our mind that this is a death sentence. As I looked into her eyes, I knew this woman sitting in front of me is an exemplary strong woman. I recall she even travelled and said to me she is not going to allow anything to stop her 'living her life'.

The book is revealing, emotional, full of demonstration of God's faithfulness and mercy, friendship, and extraordinary strength of a Christian woman. I say kudos to you, and I will recommend it to everyone, not only women, and encourage them to buy more than one copy and spread the news that death has been swallowed up. He is a defeated foe. The book of Hebrews Chapter 2: 14-15 says Jesus

14

"...Himself likewise shared in the same, that through death He might destroy him who had the power of death, that is, the devil, and release those who fear of death were all their lifetime subject to bondage."

I can say boldly that Pastor Olufunke demonstrated the character of an Evangelist throughout. She is a great example and sharing the good news of Christ even whilst being afflicted. As I witness her Sunday dances at the altar, I feel encouraged that she is indeed a woman of God. She never allowed her state of ill-health to take away her smile and laughter, putting the devil to shame that she indeed has been crucified with Christ.

I pray affliction will not rise the second time, and through this book, the Lord will win souls and heal many.

REV TAYO AROWOJOLU

Snr Pastor, New Covenant Church Edmonton, London UK

Foreword

I love this book! Though it deals with a difficult subject, it pulsates with life and energy. Pastor Olufunke writes as if she is your best friend sitting with you in your living room.

We go through a two-year tsunami; from the shock of diagnosis and the fears of an untimely death, to the trauma of surgery and chemo. We read of sleepless nights and the effect of 'Scary C' on finances and family. It is a disarmingly honest read as we journey with Olufunke and her supporters through the trials, tears, and tribulations of a body out of her control.

Thank God it's a story with a happy ending. It's a story interwoven with the love of God, the love of her family, and the unfailing support of her friends and church family.

"Weeping may endure for a night, but joy comes in the morning."

She learned first-hand that the Lord indeed 'forgives all our iniquities and heals all our diseases.' Psalm 103 verse 3

We should be grateful to her friend Stella Maris Oji encouraging Olufunke to write this book. It's a book everyone should read. As one testimonial says, "I could not put this book down until I had finished."

Olufunke does not just survive the Scary C. She emerges a vibrant, joyful woman of God who radiates His glory to everyone who meets her. This book will bless you and all who read it. It will take away fear and point you to your Creator who loves you. My prayer is that it will go far and wide.

Kate Jinadu

Director Covenant Women International Founder Liberty – making people free New Covenant Church

Introduction

No one should ever go through the Scary C journey, even though this book is written mainly for Women, but I repeat no one is ever permitted to go through the Scary C. This journey is very lonely, unpleasant, very scary but hey, I went through it and to God's glory I survived. Let me prepare you, it's not a walk in the park, I survived and am sharing my experience to help someone out there.

You are probably asking yourself…What is the Scary C?

The Scary C used throughout this book by the author refers to Cancer. I am a breast cancer survivor, and in this book, I will be referring to Cancer as the C word.

I am writing this book from my own personal experience of this Scary C word journey, and I would like to share my experience with women going through this ordeal to help them navigate and manage their way through this Scary journey. I do not have all the answers or solution or the step-by-step instructions, but I believe sharing my experience and how I dealt with it will debunk your mindset, rekindle hope, reignite the zeal and power to fight it and never give up.

This book is written with you in my mind to put a smile on your face and reenergise you for the battle ahead because you are not giving up, you are not packing it in, you will fight and survive. It's a battle and surely you will win… I won.

As a survivor, no one should ever go through the Scary C journey, it's unpleasant, overwhelming, and painful, it drains you physically, emotionally, mentally, and financially.

Breast cancer is not a death sentence… I repeat it's not a death sentence!!! It can be if you want it to be and it doesn't have to be if you don't let it. I sure did not allow it.

In this book I am going to show you how I went through this journey right from diagnosis to becoming a survivor. Reading this book will change your mindset and the defeat you might have accepted; it will also prompt you to ask yourself a major question… Do I want to live? How desperate am I?

No matter the stage you are at in this journey, or maybe you might have lost hope or the will to fight, this book is for you to refuel, recalibrate, reignite, rekindle your hope and zeal to live.

This book promises to equip you with what to expect and do during treatments, it will help you to think beyond the C word. It will help you to be in control of your emotions, moods, life and how to relate to your friends and loved ones. It will help you to understand that your life is not over. This book is simple to understand, free from all medical jargons, I believe Scary C patients are filled with that already from doctors.

Be hopeful, when there is life, there is hope.

I love this bible passage which says, "For there is hope for a tree, if it is cut down, that it will sprout again and that its tender shoots will not cease."

Are you that woman that has lost hope completely, you've just had the diagnosis and you don't know the way forward, or you've embarked on the journey, and you are just tired, overwhelmed...hey, you are not alone, remember I have been through it. I feel your pain, but I need you to stay strong at the same time. You can do it.

I really hope this book helps you, by putting a smile on your face as you journey through.

You are beautiful! Say to yourself, I am beautiful. Never ever forget that.

CHAPTER ONE

The Defining Moment

I sat spellbound like a statue, unable to move. The world seemed to have suddenly ended abruptly!! Goose bumps on my skin, voices fading away, eyes staring at me, suddenly it felt like I was alone in an unknown place, an undesirable place. I think I may have stopped breathing, I wanted to scream but no sound was coming forth. It was just like being in the unknown. I froze, I was totally and completely frozen. At first my brain refused to function but suddenly it was flooded with endless questions... what happens to my family, how will my boys cope without me... how much time have I got left, there is still so much to be done... is this it... is this the death sentence!!! I can't recall how long I was immersed in that state, but it seemed like

22

eternity. I think the doctor's voice finally broke through my consciousness… I could hear her calling my name from what appeared to be a very long distance… "Olufunke, Olufunke, Olufunke," she called gently.

I just couldn't believe what was happening, nor could I believe that I was the one in that situation. Only a couple of years ago I lost two of my friends and a very loving auntie to the Scary C word. They all fought this dreadful ailment with everything in them, they were very committed to fighting it but lost the battle in the end. Even though they did not make it, they never gave up, they fought relentlessly till the very end. I was proud of them. Initially, I was very sad of losing these beautiful souls, but as a woman of faith myself I had so many questions, but I got comforted by God's word. They fought it and now they are resting in His bosom. Guess what beautiful ladies… I HATE CANCER WITH A PASSION.

Whilst still coming to terms with all these losses, Scary C word strikes again without a warning, unfortunately this time it was me!!! I repeat it was ME!!! Can you believe this? This was real. I have just been diagnosed with the Scary C word. I was diagnosed with stage 2 breast cancer on the 23rd of June 2016.

At first, I thought it was a dream. I desperately wanted somebody to wake me up from this bad nightmare… but, it wasn't a dream, it was a stark reality staring at me. I had just been diagnosed with the horrible Scary C word, treatment plan was being put into place, appointments with oncologist and other doctors were being made, it was all like a roller coaster, everything was just happening very fast around me. This was such a horrible pill to swallow… a very bitter truth to accept. I was just empty; I had never felt such emptiness in my life before. I continued watching the consultant and the breast team and my sister, agreeing on dates and next steps but my thoughts were far away, staring into space and asking myself what do I do now? That was the question on my mind, what do I do, who do I tell or share this with, what does the future hold for me, if there was any? I had this mental or visual picture of my children popping up in front of me and I was so frightened asking myself if I really wanted to put them through this, my younger child was turning ten and getting ready for secondary school, how would he feel, my two older boys will they be able to cope, my siblings, oh no everyone has their own problems to deal with… This was a scary problem or challenge that I must deal with, but how?

Losing those beautiful people of mine, for some time I fed my thoughts or rather my mind was filled with thoughts of the Scary C word. I could not shake it off my thoughts, I wanted to find out more about the C word.

There are over two hundred different types of cancer. Knowing the Scary C type, your doctors decide on the best treatment for you. Breast cancer is one of the leading causes of cancer death in women globally. This cancer starts in the breast tissue, 1 in 7 women in the United Kingdom will develop breast cancer in their lifetime. Breast cancer can

24

be invasive or non-invasive (in- situ). It can cause different types of symptoms, for example lumps. A breast lump is the most common symptom of breast cancer. It starts when cells in the breast begin to divide, grow in an unusual and uncontrollable way. It can start in different parts of the breast; the most common type of breast cancer starts in the ducts.

By now you are asking yourself what are ducts by the way? Ducts are tubes in the breast that carry breast milk to the nipple. Breast cancer is a concern for all women; it is a disease that can and does affect women of all ages. And yet, it is particularly prevalent in older women, every year over 15,000 women aged over 70 are diagnosed with the Scary C word.

Research also shows the age range to be from 40 years old, but recently younger women from 30 years old are being diagnosed with Scary C. Although, the older you are the higher the risk and more vulnerable you are. Moreover, the outcomes for older women are worse than the younger ones.

Breast cancer does not only affect women. Men can also be affected because they also have breast tissue. It is rare and about 100 times more common among women. Men have been advised to do breast self-examination periodically and report anything unusual to their doctors. Matthew Knowles, music producer and father to Beyonce Giselle Knowles-Carter an American singer and actress, also said, "black men are diagnosed with breast cancer at a fifty two percent higher rate than white men." For the purpose of this book, I am concentrating on women, and I am also writing from my experience as a breast cancer survivor.

Breast cancer is likely caused by a combination of our genes, hormonal factors for example starting your period early under the age of twelve or having a late menopause, environment, and lifestyles. According to the World Health Organisation (WHO), changes in lifestyle, such as unhealthy diets, insufficient physical activity, use of tobacco and harmful use of alcohol, have all contributed to the increasing Scary C burden. We cannot confidently say that this is the specific CAUSE but there are things you can do to lower your chances of getting it. The sole purpose of this book is to focus on how to go through the Scary C word journey and come out victorious. It's a scary journey: I went through it but guess what, it does not have to be scary.

CHAPTER TWO

Bumpy Road Lies AHEAD

As a child growing up with an older brother, I would imitate or do whatever he did, forgetting I am a girl and I played rough but there was always a price to pay for it. From falling and hurting myself, to bumping my head or even sustaining a cut that required me to attend the hospital for stitches. This became a pattern and I guess with my frequent visits to the hospital; I developed a dislike for hospitals. My tummy turns every time I visit the hospital and I believe there was just this hospital smell that my brain associates with hospitals; its antiseptic, a little bitter, with undertones of the artificial fragrance contained in soaps and cleaners. On patient floors, the smells become intense and diverse. The hospital smells like life and death. This smell really gets me and makes me feel sick.

27

Hence, I really don't like hospitals. As a mother of three, having my babies in the hospital then, I was usually out the next one to two days. Little did I know that the hospital will become more like my second home for two years! In the space of the two years, I alternated between four different hospitals depending on what treatment I was having at the time. In fact, my entire life revolved around the hospital, hospital appointments letters from the consultant and oncologist, became my everyday mails. It sounds bumpy, right? Yes, I can confirm that it was indeed bumpy... So, brace yourself for it.

It was a lovely morning, but I was in the waiting lounge in the hospital waiting to see the oncologist with my ever-faithful hubby right by my side. It was precisely the second week after the diagnosis, meeting the oncologist shed more light on the situation and prepared me for the tough days ahead and I also had the opportunity to confirm the treatment plan recommended for me and everything was explained to me step by step and I also had to give consent.

Everything was happening very fast, like a roller coaster. Following the diagnosis, I have been very quiet and tearful, not really having the will to talk, have just been nodding and saying yes to what hubby has been saying in the past two weeks and here I am about to face the blueprint of a bumpy and scary journey which honestly scared me. I wasn't really processing it in my brain, I was just scared, angry and petrified, the fear took over my thoughts, but I wasn't sharing my thoughts. The voice of the breast consultant from the diagnosis continued to play in my head, I couldn't shake it out of my brain... I kept hearing it again, and again..." I am so sorry Olufunke, it's not good news, your result came back..." going back to the day of diagnosis, it was as if my world ended right in front of me.

The session with the oncologist was very informative, the breast team care was present too, they were the team to support me all the way through the Scary C journey, my hubby was asking all the questions. I was watching and listening, it was a bit too much for me especially when the oncologist went through all the side effects, few of which I was aware of... but guess the one that tripped me the most? It was.... losing my hair... **Noooooo**, I couldn't bear the thought. It was also a time to decide if I was happy with the treatment plan, what were the possible benefits and disadvantages of the treatment, or if I wanted another medical opinion. The decision was all mine and I had to give my consent by signing a voluminous form, so treatment could begin. I looked at my hubby and with mixed emotions, and unsteady hands, I signed the form, it felt like I had just signed my life away. The flood of questions kept pouring; how bumpy and scary would this journey be? Will I really survive it? What if I don't? Tough questions with no answers invaded my brain as I signed the form with tears in my eyes. Suddenly I asked a question, all eyes were on me waiting to hear what I was about to say. As the tears were rolling down, I looked straight at the oncologist and asked if I was allowed to travel out in the next couple of days, deferring the treatment start date. He wasn't happy with that, he explained why I shouldn't and why it's important I start treatment immediately which was all understandable, but I wasn't changing my mind! I was going, it was my sister's wedding I wasn't going to let her down and Scary C word won't take that from me. At this stage I felt it was taking over my life, I wasn't thinking of the repercussion of not starting my treatment, I was just looking forward to being with my entire family, to see my mum especially. I guess the little girl inside me just yearned for her mum. This was too overwhelming. The oncologist brought out my signed form and wrote on the top in Uppercase letter. "PATIENT DECLINED START DATE" and I signed it again. Was it the right thing to do, I don't know but hey I was travelling, attending the wedding, and spending time with my family and if I am still alive, I will start my treatment on my return. Sounds crazy, isn't it? But hey it's my life, my decision. Of course, I didn't know if it was the best decision at the time. It was a good escape for me not to focus on the scary report, thinking it will just disappear.

My treatment was put on hold following my request, set to commence on my return. Understandably, the oncologist and my hubby were not happy with the 'rash' decision. Believe me guys from diagnosis to that very moment it felt like I was in a trance, was very tearful, not sleeping well, just staring into space mostly not processing anything. Few days after my appointment with my oncologist, I was booked for another biopsy which I decided to attend by myself, it was a painful procedure, I felt so much alone and the reality and the magnitude of Scary C word finally dawned on me, sitting at the entrance of the breast care lobby at the hospital, without a care I cried my heart out, I felt broken, how bumpy and painful is the journey going to be?

Whilst crying, I heard my name, I looked up, amidst my tears I saw the face of the breast care matron looking at me, extending her hands to me to stand up and come with her into her office. In the matron's office I continued to cry uncontrollably, she said, "Olufunke it is okay to cry, please cry whenever you need to cry," and then she looked straight at me and said, "years after years I've seen women come in and out of here some stay strong and they fight it, while some don't even try to put up a fight and they are defeated already. Olufunke, which one are you going to be?" She asked. "Think about it, while you attend your sister's wedding and let me see the response in action when you start your treatment."

It was like an Angel sent to me. "Olufunke, what is it going to be? Are you going to fight this or not? Are you going to allow this deadly ailment to take control of your life?" she asked again. There and then, I decided to fight.

Hell No!!!!

I made the biggest decision to fight Scary C with God on my side. That meeting marked a turning point. The road ahead was sure a bumpy one, but I was not goanna cave in. No!

31

I made the biggest decision to fight
Scary C with God on my side.
Olufunke Ogunmodede

CHAPTER THREE

Bracing the Storm

I will Live and not Die…. Psalm 118:17

It is not a dream nor am I in a trance. I have been diagnosed with breast cancer, making me a Scary C patient. I was a breast cancer patient or a cancer patient with a treatment plan in place about to face the unknown.

Cancer treatment is typically the most difficult aspect of the Scary C word journey. Many people are frightened at the idea of having cancer treatments, particularly because of the side effects. Yes, the side effects are overwhelming on their own, but it can be managed and controlled by medicines. Treatment given varies depending on individual's

33

situation, the size of the lump, the stage of the cancer, how aggressive the cancer is, how advanced and how it has spread to other parts of the body. The treatments aim to cure the cancer but in situations where it can't cure, it controls it, this is where patients must decide whether they are going ahead with it or not. Really, going for the treatment and the side effects without any benefit is difficult. There are also cases that they had the right treatment plan in place, but their body wasn't responding, or they just can't deal with the treatment, different individuals with different experiences and results. Individual's treatment plan varies, for some the treatments can be spaced out while for some it follows consecutively.

On my Scary C journey, I met different beautiful ladies on the same journey but with different treatments and experiences. There are many different types of treatment but for this book and based on my experience I will focus on my treatment plan which was Chemotherapy, Surgery and Radiotherapy. None of this treatment is a walk in the park, trust me. This treatment is not a respecter of your ethnic background, age, or status quo. While putting my story together, I investigated famous celebrities that have survived the Scary C journey and their various experiences, so be comforted that you are not alone. Whatever you might be going through survivors of breast cancer have gone through it, it wasn't easy, but they fought it and didn't give up. No matter how painful, unbearable, and scary the treatments were, they didn't give up. I have taken the privilege to share the experiences of a few of the survivors below.

34

Angelina Jolie original name Angelina Jolie Voight, American actress and director known for her edginess as well as for her humanitarian work, at the age of 37, test revealed that she had a high risk of developing breast cancer, she underwent mastectomy surgery. She told New York times **"I wanted to write this to tell other women that the decision to have a mastectomy was not easy. But it is one I am very happy that I made. I can tell my children that they don't need to fear they will lose me to breast cancer."**

Olivia Newton-John is a bright. - Australian singer, songwriter, actress, entrepreneur, and activist, she has been a long-time activist for environmental and animal rights issues, diagnosed twice at ages 44 and 64, coping with nausea, she underwent a modified radical mastectomy and a year of chemo, herbs, acupuncture, and mental imaging.

"I visualised the chemicals as gold liquid going through my body, healing me, rather than what it really is, which is poison."

In 2013 facing the disease a second time, speaking to CBS Sunday morning, she said,

"I am happy, I'm grateful, I'm lucky. I have much to live for and I intend to keep on living."

Christina Applegate is an American actress, dancer, and producer, diagnosed at age 36, cancer was detected in one breast but underwent double mastectomy. She said on Good Morning America.

"Sometimes I cry, sometimes I scream, and I get angry, I think it's part of healing."

Chemotherapy is a type of treatment for cancer. It uses special drugs to kill Scary C cells in the body, some types of cancer can be treated with just chemotherapy, while it's also used with other treatments like radiotherapy and surgery. It may shrink your cancer or slow down its growth, which may help you live longer and help with your symptoms. There are lots of different types of chemotherapy drugs, you are being given a different mixture depending on what type of cancer you have, I was given a mixture of it. The drugs travel through the body in your blood, they work by damaging the cancer cell so that they cannot spread and make more cancer cells. Chemotherapy has its advantages and disadvantages; it does its work but kills other healthy cells in the body and the effects of this cause side effects like fatigue or nausea. It's highly recommended but it's not a must. There is a long list of side effects which can be scary, some people will only have a few, while others may have more, everyone with a different experience.

Through this Scary C word journey, I discovered it affects people differently, few are not seeing the expected result some people decline instantly, some are not too certain, some are indifferent, they don't know what to really expect apart from the long list of side effects. The two main ways Chemo is administered are by tablets or capsules and injection. I had the injection, which is putting the drugs into your blood through your skin using a needle, a small tube is put under my skin

36

which stays there all the way through the treatment. Chemotherapy was a tough, horrible, traumatic, and painful experience on its own, but I got through it and so can you. Trust me, it wasn't easy, my skin reacted to it, peeling off, but all restored now, I am so grateful to God.

My first day of Chemotherapy... I was met by lovely nurses, who attended to me, directing, and assisting me. I was very nervous but everyone in the room had a welcoming smile that was reassuring. While I waited for my turn, I watched everyone undergoing treatment, their loved ones sitting next to them, holding hands, and chatting away, watching the television, or just reading their magazines or books, it was like a different world in there... I guess it was a place where we all understood the ordeal we were going through, the pain and crazy thoughts going on in our individual brains. Looking round the room, the ambience was very calm, and I could see many clean shaved heads, I still had my wig in place, even though underneath the wig was also a shaved head. I didn't want to watch my hair fall off bit by bit, that would have been very depressing for me...my lovely hair. I loved my hair, but it really doesn't define me, so I decided to shave it off after my meeting with my oncologist, before commencing the treatment. It did reduce the anxiety, I believe preparing your mind and yourself before the treatment is very important, it helped me, remember this was my own experience. One great lesson I learnt from this ordeal was like face it squarely and think like a soldier going to war and we both know that a soldier prepares ahead no matter the outcome.

37

Chemotherapy takes everything in you, people will ask you why do you have to do this knowing all the side effects that comes with it? Hey, I wanted results, I wanted to live, that was my big why. I often think back and ask myself... hey girl, Chemo was painful. How on earth did you pull through the pain? I had six months of Chemo making it 8 treatments. Initially after my first three treatments, I still managed to go to work for a few weeks before taking a break. It wasn't easy but I pushed myself.

My job at the time gave me a sense of purpose but unfortunately, I couldn't continue as the dose became stronger, my body became weaker, I had to stop work. I can confidently tell you over and over to get yourself ready for whatever treatment plan you have in place. There are so many side effects from chemo, whichever one you are having, always find a way to manage it otherwise it depresses you. I had to deal with sores on my tongue, weak joints, fatigue, hot flushes, doctors finding my veins before each treatment, the upper side of my palm the skin was constantly peeling off, countless blood count, the veins on my left hand dried up, the list goes on, so was I looking forward to it every month the answer is No, even though I had eight treatments in six months and this was just the beginning, after this was surgery then radiotherapy, girl! It takes two years of your life at least, but some defer it, and it takes longer. You might ask why defer it? The truth is with Scary C journey you do whatever is best for YOU, Beautiful... because it is scary.

Surgery is treatment by cutting part of the body tissue, the surgeon removes all or part of the cancer. I had five different surgeries to this body of mine in a year, no one wants to go under the knife, but I had a strong why... I wanted to live. You might be asking why five in such a short time. To reduce the operating hours for mastectomy and reconstruction, I first had surgery to the lymph nodes in my armpit, then mastectomy and immediate breast reconstruction, for my reconstruction I needed tissues from my lower abdomen (tummy), for others it might be from their back, thighs, or buttocks. Your surgeon will always advise you. I had breast reduction on the other breast to balance the two, alongside this I had liposuction on my two sides following the effects of taking tissue from my abdomen.

Scary, isn't it? Each surgery has its time of healing depending on your body and skin, I believe. Even though you are given an estimated time of healing, your body might take longer to heal than the estimated time. The doctor estimates six weeks and it turns out to be nine weeks or more, you must be prepared for this.

Radiotherapy uses high energy X-rays to destroy cancer cells, while doing as little harm as possible to normal cells, normal cells can also be damaged, which may cause side effects. The good news about it is it reduces the risk of breast cancer coming back to the area it was given. To do this you must be able to move your arm freely from previous surgery, I had physiotherapy sessions for me to be able to do this, also had a support instructor from Cancer Macmillan who was placed in my

SURVIVING THE SCARY C | Olufunke Ogunmodede

local gym, such a caring lady. I also suffered from itching weeks after the radiotherapy which they refer to as late effects, I had to cover my neck and upper body with calamine lotion. If you have doubts speak with your cancer doctor or specialist doctor.

As you are about to finish this page or chapter, please give yourself a hug and say to yourself: I am beautiful, I can do this. This is what I say to myself every time and it gets me going, it helps me not to see myself any differently or think of myself any less. This journey is very overwhelming and **scary** I know, but you can do it.

CHAPTER FOUR

You are not an island

No man is an island. This is very true; this expression is a quotation from John Donne's Devotions (1624). John Donne was an English poet, one of the greatest of English prose.

Humans are supposed to support one another, as in you cannot manage this all by yourself. Let me start by saying you cannot manage Scary C word by yourself, you need your loved ones.

At the beginning of the Scary C ordeal, I struggled with sharing the sad news with my children and siblings. I believe I was being strong for them, trying to shield or protect them from the agony of the news, but

41

through the entire Scary C journey I now know better. My decision to not share with my children immediately was causing more confusion for them, even though I was trying all my best to stay strong, but they could observe the changes, the frequent visits to the hospital, the medication, it was a long list of things. I wasn't sure of how they would cope, and I guess I didn't want them to ask me questions that I might not have the answers to at that time.

At the early stage of treatment, it was a bit manageable but as treatment was progressing, I couldn't hold things together, couple of times I have fallen down my steps because of the chemotherapy effect on my bladder and joints, my hubby used to help me up but on this faithful day, he wasn't around, and I fell down the steps… Guess who helped me up…my second son, I never knew he was that strong, but I was glad he was able to help me up, he was caring and very supportive, checking on me as often as he could on that day which was so comforting to me. My eldest would ask me about the injections in the fridge…. too many questions, I had to tell them that I wasn't strong, that I was unwell but soon I will be well, nothing for them to worry about. My eldest wasn't going down with what I said, he spoke to me afterwards that he is a big boy that I should tell him, that he could handle it, so I told him, it was like a weight lifted off me, he was calm and very reassuring. He said, "Mum you will beat this," which I did but at that time…. I was unsure. Guess what!! He composed a music about me going through cancer and he was able to express his feelings which was very comforting to me.

42

Oh!! My youngest was really playing up in school, he had all these sad stories he told his friends at school and all the mums were all asking after me from my hubby. On this very day myself and my youngest boy were watching the television, a Macmillan advert came up, it usually makes me tearful, but I held it together, suddenly, my boy with his eye fixed on the screen said, "Mum, is that like you?" referring to the woman with the shaven head in the advert. I responded, "Yes," and he looked at me and gave me a hug. I believe in his own little way he was asking me if I was going through the C word, with my similar shaved head.

It was great letting the boys in, they were caring and helpful, showed good understanding of my different mood swings. They handled the situation in their own ways, which made me very proud of them. So, there were less questions from them, especially seeing loads of mail from the hospital, they understood what was going on and they did their best. I also did the same with my siblings, my two sisters and my younger brother, I didn't share with them at the beginning but shared with my older brother. As I said in the previous chapter, I didn't want to trouble them, I was thinking that they had enough on their plate and not adding mine to theirs, but I was so wrong.

Really, I didn't know how to break it to them, but I eventually did with the support of my adopted big sister Sis Eny, yes, I refer to her as my adopted big sister. I can't begin to tell you why, but all you need to know is she is beautiful in and out. She has always been a pillar of support for me and was right there with me from diagnosis till the end of ordeal. She is a very busy woman, a pastor, entrepreneur, a mother but guess what with all her tight schedules, she would come with me for chemotherapy treatment which takes basically more than ten hours, she would hold my hand through it, those were priceless moments and it makes you understand why you need your loved ones around, you can't just be an island, going through the Scary C journey. I believe we deal with issues or pain in different ways, for me sometimes I stay stronger dealing with things in a conserved way, while I went to work from diagnosis to middle of chemotherapy, I only shared with my managers, they were supportive, the workload was reduced I didn't share with my colleagues, but they were aware that I was very unwell but didn't know the full details, don't get me wrong my colleagues are loving and caring, I didn't share with them at that time because that was the only way I could keep myself together and not be tearful every minute someone was talking to me. I love you guys, if any one of you is reading this book.

The first 6 months of the Scary C journey, I was so tearful, I cried so much. You are not alone if you are tearful, it gets better.

As an early year professional, I work with children between the ages of zero to five, I needed to stay strong not to break down in front of the little ones. But along the line I was becoming weaker, tired, and fatigued. Once a little girl at my workplace came to sit next to me during one of the outdoor activities, she asked me if I was tired. "Are

44

you tired, Olufunke?" A tear rolled down, I quickly brushed it away and pretended as if I was brushing a fly away. I replied no but she still gave me one of her little hugs, bless her heart.

Family is key, I cannot but over emphasize the importance of family! My siblings and their partners, believe me they rock. Even though I shared with them in the middle of treatment they were still amazing. They gave me their undivided attention, which also helped my hubby, it became a shared burden, from my experience you need them every step of this Scary C journey. I didn't have to worry about preparing food, it was all taken care of, and their company was ever priceless, when they would come visiting me at home or the hospital, it was refreshing and reassuring, they bring this energy with them, that strengthened me to fight this battle. Every little help counts, please try not to say *no* to any help offered. Having my sisters on board brought me joy as well as grief, sounds confusing, doesn't it? It is simple, because we are all sisters, they needed to get tested too. I was scared they both had to take the BRCA test, as weak as I was, I had to encourage them as the big sister, but I was deeply scared for them, I had to stay strong for them. The results were good and not good, one had all clear and the other was positive.

At this point I believe you want to scream out loud; **Nooooooooo!!!!!!!!!!!!** Go ahead and scream as I did when I was told.

I hate Scary C word with passion. No one should ever go through this ordeal but if you are going through it, sum up all your courage and

45

energy and fight it without any mercy. If you are a survivor, don't ever for one minute give up on your dreams. Dream big, you can do it!

CHAPTER FIVE

Your thought tank What are your thoughts so far, beautiful?

Scary C word is a life changing ailment, and every survivor has their unique journey and basically have different stories to tell but one thing that matters most from my own experience is to be very intentional about taking control of your thoughts. From the very first day of diagnosis, it is very important for you to be in control of your words and thoughts.

When you are in control of your thoughts, it helps you to think and plan regardless of the diagnosis or situation at hand, but if you are not, fear sets in and takes over, and you are a mess.

47

The bible teaches us in the second book of Timothy1:7... *For God has not given us a spirit of fear, but of power and of love and of a sound mind.*

At the beginning of the Scary C journey, I allowed the fear of the diagnosis to take over, all I did initially was cry, cry, cry and feel sorry for myself and make many bad decisions.

Everything was like a roller coaster, a death sentence with a timeline hanging on my neck but once I decided to be in charge, changing my mindset that I am victorious, and I will not be defeated, I will not let Scary C word take over my life, I will fight it and God will see me through.

Scary C word takes everything from you, emotionally it drains you, that's more reason you must pick yourself up and move on despite all the odds. You might be asking how can I do this, have you seen the state I am lately, how can I be in control in this scary and overwhelming journey? My answer is YES! YES! you can Beautiful, don't be intimidated by Scary C word, be in control. I started by taking baby steps of saying positive things to myself, I began to protect my internal conversation, I began to do the opposite of what my mind was saying, I started preparing my mind before the treatment. As I mentioned in chapter three, I had my hair shaved off before the treatment and I told myself repeatedly, affirming that I am beautiful. During the treatment with the steroid intake, I blew up in weight and whenever negative and crazy thoughts invaded my brain, I would look in the mirror and tell myself: I am beautiful.

48

There was this faithful day I felt good and decided to go to work... Guess what? I didn't make it beyond the train station when my joint and ankle caved in, and I nearly fell over. It was unbelievable and instinctively without being told, I knew I had to give up work completely and concentrate on my treatment and getting well. With this realisation, I became anxious with all the thoughts running wild in my head! How was I going to cope not doing anything? What was I going to do without work? Fear gripped. Suddenly I thought I was going to be a burden to everyone. But I had to forge ahead regardless; I had to let go of work, I had to embrace staying at home, even though my going to work gave me a sense of purpose but my 'Why' to live was stronger.

I do understand how difficult it is to stay positive in this scary situation, a situation where your body is falling apart, you don't know what to expect when you wake up each day. There were days I woke up with a swollen face, my cheeks all sore, sensitive, and painful. Even on days like this, I learnt to smile and affirm that I am strong and healed. Naturally I am a bubbly person full of energy and smiles, but I became very sad after the diagnosis which I later changed by developing a positive mindset. I surrounded myself with positive thinking people, people who were very encouraging and didn't entertain pity party, I began to live each day as if it's the last, enjoying every minute of it, doing things I love doing, listening to good refreshing music, watching movies, having a me time, eating healthy and best of all was making my different smoothies. I seized the moment as the time to explore

49

different types of smoothies and believe me it was my first time doing this and was very rewarding.

I stopped focusing on the Scary C word, whenever I go for my treatment. I stopped looking sad and began to try to look good. Naturally, I am someone who enjoys looking good; I would slap my makeup on looking pretty without any care! On a couple of times at the hospital, other patients thought I was a doctor that was just checking on them. Very funny isn't it, I refused to let Scary C define me. I joined small group sessions and contributed to conversations especially when I have my family around, I will have a good laugh with them. I stopped pitying myself, I embraced their love and support, tried new things, basically doing things that make me happy, whatever brings a smile to my face.

I must emphasise that all this wasn't happening right at the beginning. I had my moments of 'self-pity' and the why me whining', in fact it took me several weeks into treatment before I started having a change of mindset, but it can be different for you especially if you have just been diagnosed. My advice would be, 'Please don't focus on the diagnosis too much, fill your thoughts with your exit plans and continue to tell yourself that you can beat this and surely, you will, or you shall.

On this Scary C journey, I joined several support groups and related online with women that were diagnosed with stage 4 Scary C. I saw first-hand how they managed it positively, they were brave and strong, living their life and very determined to fight it regardless of the negative report they got. I believe this also gave me the willpower to live and face each day as it comes. I think to beat this scary ailment, you really must be intentional and deliberate about being positive amidst all the chaos. There were times I could have had a long day in the hospital, which was really depressing, but instead of focusing on the pain, tiredness, the test itself, I would go straight to a nice restaurant and treat myself to something new and special, having a Me time, it does relax me, taking my mind off things.

It's also great to have a diary and write down how you are feeling at a particular moment, especially a few days after chemotherapy treatment, what are your thoughts, what are you feeling, how are you managing it? A few days after any chemo treatment, my tongue is always covered with sores which makes eating very painful. Knowing this, I will practically stay off spicy food that will burn my tongue and stick to very bland food, horrible but I refuse to be miserable. I was in control. Stay positive, speak positive and think positive, you will surely defeat Scary C. Be kind to yourself...Beautiful!

Whichever stage you are at, stop focusing on the Scary C word, live each day as the last, fill your thoughts with nice thoughts, think about places you would like to visit and imagine yourself on their beach having fun, keep the hope alive. Maybe you have dreams that have not manifested yet, begin to picture them happening and ending well. Focus

51

on things that can bring you joy and put a smile on your face. I know it's hard, you can do it.

As a woman of faith, I believe in the word of God that says I can do all things through Christ who strengthens me. (Philippians 4:13 NKJV)

What are you going to do?

CHAPTER SIX

MY FAITH

Faith is the substance of things hoped for, the evidence of things not seen. (Hebrews 11:1)

What has faith got to do with this, you might be thinking? I love this old song by Tina turner an American Singer, which says, "What's Love got to do with it" just as we are saying what's faith got to do with Scary C journey.

As a survivor and a woman of faith, for me faith had and still has a big part to play in the Scary C journey. If you are not a woman of faith, it's fine, just roll with me.

"The cancer journey was tough and at the same time easy and interesting. Tough in the sense that the aftermath of every chemo

53

session was horrific and painful. Easy and interesting because God strengthened me all through. The support of friends and family was overwhelming. In other words, "I survived cancer because God said he was not done with me yet, and he also surrounded me with wonderful friends and families to hold me through the journey." Mrs Nike Diyaolu was a group head Human Resources administrator. She is a good friend of mine, in 2011 she was diagnosed with stage 4 breast cancer. She trusted in God for total healing and God strengthened her through the horrific journey and she is testifying that God kept her. In my journey I can relate to this testimony that it was just God all the way! The Scary C journey is very stormy but when you trust and have faith in God it goes a long way. My faith in God gave me the assurance that God was with me all the way. Of course, as expected, I was very sad initially. I was full of pity for myself, I was frustrated, depressed, couldn't believe it nor comprehend it. I was taken over by fear and disbelief but throughout the journey it was so evident that God was with me. I can boldly testify that God made adequate provisions for me during the ordeal. You might ask what do I mean?

What I am simply saying is that God surrounded me with amazing people, friends and families that were just super-duper amazing. Even when I was fearful, and allowing all these negative thoughts to torment me, there where instances my adopted big sister would call me to pray with me or keep me on the call, while she plays awesome worship songs like "I have learnt to trust in him through it all" by Andrae Crouch an American gospel singer and songwriter. These songs lifted my soul and gave me hope. My spiritual parents were also constantly praying for me, my husband and families also praying along, all this increased my faith more and more and gave me the hope that God will see me through the Scary C journey, and I am totally grateful to God.

There were times when the pain was just unbearable and indescribable and I won't be able to sleep, my husband will try all he can do but the pain would persist, and he will go down on his knees to pray for me. And believe it or not after a few minutes, I would experience calmness around me, and I will fall asleep.

I am a woman of faith and I believe in divine health and divine healing as part of God's promises for myself and family and his words say, "by his stripes I am healed."

But he was wounded for our transgressions, he was bruised for our iniquities; the chastisement for our peace was upon him, and by his stripes we are healed. Isaiah53:4 NKJV

I was able to find my path of believing and trusting in God's promises after the diagnosis with the support and help of the amazing people whom God surrounded me with and I held on to God's word. When I shared the sad news with my spiritual father PTA, his question to me was, "Do you believe you are healed by his stripes?" I paused and answered, "Yes, I do believe."

You might be saying that some who are not of any faith get healed, they do survive this journey, I get it totally but for my experience I ascribe

55

all glory to God for seeing me through all the way. There were days it was very painful; words cannot describe the excruciating pain I experienced during the different treatments, but I held on to confessing and affirming God's word and promises and it helped me. The first two days after the reconstruction surgery were the worst and most painful. I could not move my body; it was painful and scary. I was constantly pressing on the morphine pain medication button next to me and I screamed unbearably. The more I screamed, the more the morphine…believe me, nothing could really take the pain away completely, the morphine just numbs it for a few hours, then wears off but God had sustained me. He is always indeed a present help. During the Scary C journey, I have seen people that gave up instantly and people that didn't want to have the treatment and people whose body wasn't responding to the treatment and gave up. My trust was not in all the treatment given but my trust was in the God of the medicine.

Please understand that going under the knife is not a walk in the park, for me it was just like going into the unknown, you have your body all marked up by the surgeon and you are surrounded by all these strange friendly faces in blue and green, with their heads and hands covered. As you confirm your name and date of birth, you are being given the anesthetic and before you know it, you are slipping into an unconscious zone, and you are left at the hands of those strange people… What happens in fourteen hours you really don't know, that was my longest hours for mastectomy and reconstruction and gaining consciousness back in about two hours. I believe God's presence was with me all the way, from the beginning to the end. In my diary I noted it down in the early hours of leaving home for the surgery, a sister of mine called me, prayed with me, and reminded me that The Lord is my shepherd, and all was well and as I was wheeled to the theatre, I continued to affirm the Lord is my shepherd, I shall not fear. As a child back then, growing up in a Christian family, this was one of my favorite Psalms from the bible, we constantly recite it at home and in Sunday school.

You might not be of any faith or neither a Christian, but as you are reading this book kindly pause a minute and recite my favorite Psalm. It's very reassuring and comforting.

The lord is my shepherd; I shall not want. He makes me to lie down in green pastures; he leads me besides the still waters. He restores my soul; he leads me in the paths of righteousness for his name's sake. yea, though I walk through the valley of the shadow of death, I will fear no evil; for you are with me; your rod and your staff, they comfort me. You prepare a table before me in the presence of my enemies; you anoint my head with oil; my cup runs over. Surely goodness and mercy shall follow me, all the days of my life; and I will dwell in the house of the lord for ever. Psalm23 NKJV

In this Scary C journey, prayer makes a huge difference. To be able to pray and have people praying constantly for you goes a long way. I experienced the tremendous impact, and it helped me through the journey. I couldn't have gone through this alone without prayers, there were times my faith was very shaky, unanswered questions but I held on to God's word and promises and his words strengthened my feeble body daily. He is a present help in the time of trouble, even when we think he's not there he is ever present to take away the pain and wipe our tears away, putting his arms around us reassuring us of his finished work on the cross. 'It is finished.' He said.

Hey beautiful one reading, I believe you will agree with me that prayers make a big difference in this scary journey especially if you are a woman of faith. As I said at the beginning of this chapter, even if you are not of faith, kindly roll with me and I will teach you how to at the end of this book.

CHAPTER SEVEN

Your lifestyle matters

Hey, beautiful!!!!! How would you describe your lifestyle? Take a minute and think about it and ask yourself if it is great or if it can be better and how you can make it better. Our lifestyle can be described as conventional unhealthy, carefree, dangerous, edgy, stressful, completely vegetarian, intense, comfortable, unhurried, traditional and many more.

The simple definition of lifestyle according to the dictionary is the way you live including your style, attitudes, and possessions. There are different types of lifestyles, but for surviving the Scary C journey we will be touching more on the active and healthy lifestyle. I do not believe there is a perfect lifestyle, where nothing can go wrong, no

59

trouble and you don't have to worry about anything, but I believe working towards a good healthy lifestyle is very achievable.

Yes! It is very achievable, to be honest I was not too conscious of a healthy lifestyle before the Scary C diagnosis but going through the journey I now understood the importance and the impact of a healthy lifestyle.

In chapter one I ended it by saying breast cancer is likely caused by a combination of our genes, hormonal factors, environment, and lifestyles. We cannot confidently say that this is the specific cause but there are things we can do to lower our chances of getting it. From my experience, maintaining a healthy lifestyle really helps to lower chances of getting it.

An active lifestyle is simply doing physical activity throughout the day. This can be any activity that gets you up and moving such as running, walking, dancing, lifting weights, swimming, steppers and using the treadmill. The list is endless, but the benefits are many, such as helping to prevent many chronic diseases such as high blood pressure, stroke, breast cancer, etc. It also manages body weight and health conditions and helps you live longer. Having regular and consistent physical activity can improve and lower the risk of developing several diseases like type 2 diabetes, cancer and cardiovascular. If you can recall at the beginning of this chapter I said before the Scary C diagnosis, I was not conscious of my lifestyle, I did engage in few physical activities, but I did it only when I felt like it, it wasn't regular and consistent. I believe I just did it when bored really. I had good intentions but was not good enough. As a young person back then I was not really into anything sporty or too physical, I would rather opt for the dressing up, fashion and drama activity, basically anything not too physical and strenuous but I loved dancing, my mum would enroll me for different dancing activities and as a grown person I would join Zumba and dance classes at a local gym.

An active lifestyle is beneficial for anyone going through a Scary C journey. For me to get through the Scary C journey I had to be very intentional about my physical activities for example like walking, I am not really a fan, I thought it was boring but instead of focusing on the boring aspect I began to focus on the impact and benefits of walking to my body. Initially I started with fifteen to twenty minutes' walk which I increased gradually daily, and I also joined cancer group organised by the Macmillan Cancer group in my local gym, in this group we had our own instructor who would guide us through basic and essential physical activities, and we would always start with fifteen minutes' walking or running on the treadmill. This was helpful especially on my joints and leg muscles, it helped preserve my sanity, kept me going especially from the heavy effect of chemotherapy. I also took up Zumba, it was not easy, but I kept pushing my body to be strong and active while going through all the treatment. The Cancer team at the hospital were incredibly supportive and they would encourage you also to join a walking group. At every stage of the treatment, you cannot afford not to have a routine of physical activity in place, this activity also helps you to regain control of your hand, your grip and other parts of your body being impaired by the treatment. It also helped me to manage my body weight and pulse, especially after being injected with steroids. I cannot but over emphasise the importance of physical activity through the C journey, please try and find time for some regular exercise for extra health and fitness benefits, aim for at least thirty minutes of physical activity every day, I know you might not feel up to it but think of the benefit and push yourself and give yourself a well done pat at the end of it.

So, what do I mean by a healthy lifestyle? A healthy lifestyle is simply a state of complete physical, emotional, mental, social, and spiritual wellbeing. It's also about eating a balanced diet, having regular exercise, getting plenty of rest and sleep, avoiding stress, limiting alcohol, and avoiding drugs and tobacco and staying at a healthy weight.

As women we should take time to look after ourselves, having the 'ME' time. Often as women we tend to look after every other person forgetting about ourselves. It is essential to find time for 'YOU'. As a woman that enjoys her life before the Scary C ordeal and still enjoys life after, I eat whatever I enjoy but not all what I enjoy is good for me. I must be extremely cautious of what I eat daily.

SURVIVING THE SCARY C | Olufunke Ogunmodede

"What you put in is what you get out." (Colonics lagos)

From my experience going through the Scary C journey, having a healthy lifestyle is particularly important and beneficial to the body. Through the Scary C journey, I understood the negative effect of all the junk food I used to consume daily.

Scary C cells have the same needs as normal cells, they need a blood supply to bring oxygen and nutrients to grow and survive.

Scary C can quickly spread to other parts of the body when it comes in contact with a catalyst that sets it off. Food is one of the primary catalysts that can cause cells to reproduce at a rapid rate, that is why it is especially important to eat a diet that consists of healthy foods only. There are foods you must avoid when going through the Scary C journey, eating the wrong food could spell disaster for your recovery process. It is important to attend small group classes with the Cancer team, where they teach you about what to and not to eat. All this I attended, and it helped me. My breast consultant also gave me a good tip about vegetables and fruits which also worked well for me. There were some habits I gave up instantly, for example I was a lover of fizzy drinks especially my beloved... you can guess the name Coca-cola, I had to substitute it for herbal tea, decaffeinated tea with almond milk or a little bit of skimmed milk. When you implement healthy food options into your diet, as you are about to start your treatment, the adverse side effects of your procedure can be offset.

There are many articles out there stating what to eat and what not to eat, articles about Cancer fighting super foods, it is particularly important to look for information or articles backed up by research from authoritative sources like Cancer research UK and world health organization. It has been proven over and over that eating the right foods with the right nutrients and vitamins helps to reduce your chances of developing specific types of Cancer.

The World Health Organisation (WHO) recommends eating at least three portions of non-starchy vegetables and two portions of fruit each day. Fruits and vegetables provide a mixture of health-promoting ingredients such as fiber, phytochemicals, vitamins, and minerals. While the World Cancer Research Fund recommends that women who have had breast Cancer follow advice to reduce their risk of recurrence. This includes eating a healthy diet that is high in fiber and low in saturated fats, being physically active, maintaining a healthy weight and limiting alcohol. Also, according to the WHO there are Cancer causing foods such as processed meat, red meat, alcohol, sugary drinks or non-diet soda and fast processed foods and there are also Cancer fighting foods which are rich in fiber, helps reduce the risk of different Cancer. Fighting foods such as fruits and vegetables, tomatoes, garlic, citrus fruits, carrots, wholegrains. Wholegrains are rich in dietary fiber, such as brown rice, oats, rye, and wholegrain bread. It is essential to eat the recommended five servings of fruit and vegetables a day. I was very intentional about my fruit and vegetable and protein, I decided to buy organic fruit and vegetables, I can testify that it made a great impact, my skin that was scaling from chemotherapy became smooth. I was not really a fruit and vegetable person but remembering my WHY to live was strong. I educated myself on the right food and I also attended sessions with Macmillan Cancer staff in the hospital. I also searched for different ways to enjoy fruit and vegetables, I also joined a 30-day challenge, the list goes on. You must find what really works for you; it puts you in control of this Scary C journey.

CHAPTER EIGHT

Financial Aspect

Money!!! Money!!!! Money!!!

It's overwhelming going through the Scary C word journey, which makes it double overwhelming, when it affects your income. The money aspect of Scary C journey is very important and a big part of the journey. In some other parts of the world, research has shown that many women are not speaking up because of the fear of the financial impact on their family and jobs, their source of income. They would rather be quiet about it, keeping everything under wrap, but this becomes even more scary and dangerous, increasing the mortality rate.

I can personally tell you from my experience finances had a big impact on my family, my job, going through Scary C. As a full time, early years professional, working nine to five from Monday to Friday, the

66

impact was huge on my job and income. As I explained earlier in the previous chapter, there were times it was just impossible to go to work, as I was in so much pain and at every stage of treatment, there was just a hurdle to cross. For example, during the chemotherapy treatment the first seven to ten days after treatment were very crucial, my immunity level became very low and to prevent any form of infection, I basically had to stay home. When my immunity level is very low, I can't be in a crowd, I can't be around people with any form of symptoms, the nature of my job is working with children. It's impossible to avoid their sneezes and running noses, cuddles and I also commute on the trains, which I had to avoid because of the overcrowding again. Basically, what I resulted to in the first three months of the chemotherapy treatment I had to be off sick the first week after the treatment, regaining my immunity level, then resume work. This was the pattern for the first three months and not forgetting all the numerous appointments with the oncologist, the breast team and consultants, scans, this had an impact on my working hours and the number of absences was more than my entitled sick leave.

As the treatment became more intensified, my body and joints became weaker and unfortunately my health forced me to stop going to work. My going to work basically generates my income in meeting my basic needs, paying bills, but at that time my going to work also gave me a sense of purpose. It had a huge impact on my income, but I had to be signed off. On this faithful morning, I struggled to get to work, I was at the train station about ten minutes from my home and I felt a very sharp pain in my ankle, I slowed down and when I tried to walk any further, I nearly fell over, it was like a dislocation of my ankle from its joint, I was so terrified. I called my hubby to pick me up, luckily, he was still home so he took me straight to the GP. As a Chemotherapy patient I was entitled to an emergency walk in at the medical Centre, my doctor wasn't really surprised with what happened to me. His question to me was, "Why are you still going to work?" So, it's just a basic knowledge that Scary C word will affect your finances, not just yours alone but the entire family. Yes, everyone in the family will be affected, husband, partner, children all inclusive, you really must be prepared for it. Scary, isn't it?

To be honest, I really didn't know what was coming or to be expected, I didn't have any plan but with you reading this book, I believe it will help you envisage and put things into perspective, you will be ready, prepared to face the challenges.

Looking back at the journey, it wasn't just one sided, income was basically down on both sides. My hubby was my main career, he had to take me to all my appointments, there were appointments, scans that I needed to have someone with me, he had to come with me and cancel his work for that day.

Having to go through Chemotherapy treatment as discussed in previous chapter was draining and overwhelming. Each time I went in for chemo, the procedure practically takes the whole day. It's very depressing if you don't have anyone by your side or with you, my hubby would take me there and sit with me, missing out on work, contracts and as a self-employed, if you don't put in the hours there is no pay. The chemo treatment lasted for six months, which was just part of the treatment, then I had regular MRI scans and surgeries, and as I said previously, I had five different surgeries on my body following chemotherapy.

So, what am I saying? Every step in Scary C word treatment you need help, I needed my hubby and his time and this in turn had a big impact on his income. When I had lymphadenectomy, also known as lymph node dissection surgery, I couldn't lift my arms, I practically couldn't do anything with my right hand for weeks and when I had the main surgery the mastectomy and reconstruction I couldn't stand straight nor walk, I had to use a frame, my hubby had to care for me, all this affected him financially and emotionally and when both incomes were affected, our children were also affected, my older boy just started in University; my youngest about to do his 11 years plus examinations, bills to be paid, basic needs, shopping, food preparation were all affected. Also, with our affected income, cost of shopping increased for example I made sure I had a balanced meal, as I had to buy only wholemeal and organic fruits and vegetables, organic skimmed milk, or any plant-based milk, all these do not come cheap.

There were also appointments that I would go to by myself, excusing my hubby to go to work, but these appointments incurred more bills, because I would have to take a cab back and forth from the hospital. There was a particular day I had a procedure and there was just too much traffic, on arriving at the hospital, there was just no space to park, he had to park and go with me upstairs because we were behind time, after meeting with the surgeon, he went back to find a better parking space.

Guess what happened??? A parking ticket has been issued, amidst all the bills and the parking fee on a regular basis, you find yourself paying for five to six hours depending on the waiting time with the doctors again.

This was where my loved ones came in with their support and care, making it easier on hubby, they will sit with me for chemo, bringing their work along as they were able to work from their laptop, enabling hubby to work. I was signed off work for more than eight months, this not inclusive of the time for appointments and recovery times, all these were way more than sickness benefits and days that I was allowed at the organisation I worked with then. The sickness pay was calculated based on my duration with the organisation, the salary or income I was paid was dependent on my number of years with the organisation and this had a huge impact on us financially.

70

Scary C word treatment cost and financial impact varies in different countries. I will touch briefly on its impact on United Kingdom, United States of America and a third world country, like Nigeria.

Research says, "In the United Kingdom, NHS on Cancer care accounted for 5.81 billion pounds equating to 5.6% of total NHS budget. France and Sweden spend 10% and 7% of their total healthcare."

What is the NHS in the UK?

The NHS is the public funded national healthcare system in the UK, which provides a comprehensive service, available to all irrespective of gender, race, disability, age, sexual orientation, religion, or belief. It stands for the National Health Services, which provides health care for all UK Citizens based on their need for medical care rather than their ability to pay.

In the UK Cancer treatment is free to people who live in the UK, but if you don't, you will have to pay. According to Research, every year over 250,000 people in England are diagnosed with Scary C word and around 130,000 dies because of the disease. The Annual NHS costs for Scary C word services are £5 billion but the cost to society, including costs for loss of productivity is 18.3 billion. More people are surviving the scary disease.

Also in the UK, you have a choice, you can either go to a private or NHS, but usually the treatments are the same. Within the private sector, you pay, and you might be able to get it done quicker. I went through the NHS, and they did a fantastic job,

The staff especially the breast care team, were all amazing. I was privileged to receive a completely free Scary C treatment package with free medications. I thank God. Whereas in the United States of America, it is a different story, where people must pay for medical services, the financial impact on people going through Scary C is overwhelming. The Scary C treatment cost an average total of $150,000. The Scary C treatments are very high, higher than treatment for other common health conditions. As Cancer survival rises so do the prices of life-saving Cancer treatments. Americans struggle with both the physical and emotional effects of high out of pocket medical costs. A very high number reported financial struggles following a Cancer diagnosis and low-income families who are uninsured or underinsured faces medical bills four times more and this is very overwhelming for the patient and the family.

Most Scary C patients mostly rely on financial support from friends and families or even source for funds from crowd funding or charity organisations like Go funding.

I personally have been privileged to be a channel of blessing to a couple of women that I know myself and through friends and families, living in the USA. But the good thing about the countries considered to be high income countries, is the decline in number of people dying from the dreadful Scary C, but this is the contrast in the third world countries, where there is low income and inflation and limited resources, there is a high rise in diagnosis and death from Scary C word.

At the beginning of this chapter, I made mention of women in some third world countries like Nigeria, who are not speaking up because of the fear of the financial impact on their families and income, they keep quiet about their diagnosis or any unusual growth, symptom, or deformity in their breasts. As a result, many die, the disease is not detected in time and the condition can be made worse, because of lack of Cancer resources and equipment. As Nigeria is part of the third world developing countries, they are low- and middle-income countries that have limited resources available to treat and detect Cancer and they also, can't afford to provide free treatment at the same time. There have been instances where Cancer patients were being treated for something totally different. Earlier in this book I made mention of a friend that I lost to Scary C word, she lived in Nigeria, became worse with treatment given to her in Nigeria and lack of equipment, by the time they flew to the UK, it was all out of control… too late.

In Nigeria, with the low income and low cost of living, high medical expenses, no free medical expenses, no jobs, women are not prepared to go for screening, nor giving up their source of income because of the big impact upon their households and themselves, they would rather be quiet about it and suffer in silence.

This year, WHO has spelt out the need to step up Cancer services in low and middle-income countries to prevent 60% increase in Scary C cases over the next two decades. Dr Tedros Adhanom Ghebreyesus, the Director- General, WHO said, "At least 7 million lives could be saved over the next decade, by identifying the most appropriate science for each country situation, by basing strong Cancer responses on universal health coverage, and by mobilizing different stakeholders to work together."

To conclude Scary C has a huge detrimental impact on victims' finances and their loved ones, it requires more resources to be managed effectively. Unfortunately, the demographics often determine the outcome of it whether the victim survives it or not. Support in place is very crucial, it determines victims' survival.

In the next chapter I will be discussing or informing you of my support while battling with Scary C.

CHAPTER NINE

My Support Groups

Everyone needs someone, we all need each other, it's great to connect.
Olufunke Ogunmodede

Supporting others according to the dictionary by Merriam webster is the act of helping someone by giving love and encouragement. Accessing help goes a long way, just like a hug speaks volume. One big lesson I learnt from going through the Scary C journey is support comes in various forms and ways. There is emotional support, financial support, physical and mental support.

What do I mean? Let's explore emotional support, whilst going through Scary C journey is undeniably overwhelming. As I have shared earlier, I was practically in tears most times, I couldn't even bring myself to have a conversation regarding Scary C without opening the tap...

75

meaning crying. Thinking back, I really pitied myself initially but if you are doing the same, please stop it...you and I ARE NOT the first to go through this journey neither are we the last, I picked myself up, I accessed help and I became hopeful again, so can you. Depending on where you live, there are many support groups out there, you find them locally and online and they are recommended by most hospitals too.

A support group provides an opportunity for people to share personal experiences and feelings, coping strategies or first- hand information about diseases or treatments. It provides invaluable spaces for members to share experiences, speak openly about challenges and share information.

At the very beginning the breast care team offered me all the information regarding accessing the right support group, to be honest I wasn't interested because that was the last thing on my mind, but one day I decided to check out a local one which I see practically on my way to the hospital, but I didn't have the guts. I pulled myself together and I stepped in, looked around, a lady with a smile on her face said hello, I replied and left instantly, told myself *No, this is not meant for me,* and I never went back. Please don't get me wrong, it was a lovely place, a welcoming place but I wasn't ready for it. Maybe this is you, don't push yourself, till you feel comfortable in whichever support you choose. My second trial and choice, I was very ready. I stumbled on it in the hospital, whilst waiting to see my oncologist, I felt at ease in there, a joint conversation was going on at the far end of the room, I was asked if I wanted to join or just to look around, I chose to sit with the group and I was blown with the conversations, everyone had few seconds/minutes to share something. I enjoyed it but I couldn't wait till the end, it was time to see my oncologist, I told myself, I really must come back here, I told the receptionist I needed to go, and she gave me all the necessary details and I was booked to come back and speak with one of the counsellors there. I felt great, it was the beginning of a new experience.

Support groups are run by trained peers and focus is on emotional support, sharing experiences and one to one support. They are very effective; it empowers people to put in more effort in solving their own problem. A good support group will leave you with a new perspective that helps you to make progress towards a health goal. It gave me more drive to fight Scary C.

What do I mean? I went back for my appointment at the foundation, everyone was lovely, I spoke with the counsellor, she was lovely, she made me understand that she knew all I was undergoing through…the emotions, anxiety, pain, and I was thinking how? Guess what, she is a survivor of dreadful Scary C, she showed me her photos and what a transformation. That moment the drive to fight was stronger, I connected with her, and she was able to counsel regarding my emotions and the symptoms, shared what worked for her, it was a big relief, the place became like my second home. To reduce any anxiety before the chemo procedure, I would book a session with them for reflexology, which was always very calming.

Worrall et al (2018) author of one door mental health – found that support groups are effective at reducing symptoms, improving social competence, and increasing healthy behaviors, self-esteem, and perceptions of overall being.

Research has shown that having a strong support system has many positive benefits such as high levels of wellbeing, better coping skills and a longer and healthier life. Studies have also shown us that support group/system can reduce depression, anxiety and stress and taking part in support group where you both give and receive help is an effective way to reduce stress and anxiety.

Macmillan Cancer support is United kingdom's leading source of Cancer support helping more and more people living with Scary C. This is a charity founded in 1911 by Douglas Macmillan. He watched his father die of Scary C and this was an inspiration for him. He founded the charity for the prevention and relief of cancer. He wanted advice and information to be provided to all people living with Scary C, homes for patients at low or no cost and voluntary nurses to attend to patients in their own homes. Today much of his legacy lives on.

Macmillan supports you right from the diagnosis, treatments, drugs after treatment as well as advice to help with the different ways Scary

C may impact one's life. They offer physical and emotional support, financial support and practical help as Cancer throws a lot one's way, they are there to listen and support. They also help with work, people losing their work and they also have an online community where you can talk to people affected by the same Scary C, blog about your experience and ask experts questions.

I was very fortunate to receive support from Macmillan support right from the beginning of diagnosis to treatment and after treatment. I joined the online community, which was awesome and attended all follow up sessions, I was assigned to a Macmillan physiotherapist who supported myself and a few others in a small group. She supported us with physical exercise and especially making use of our arms after the surgery and prepared us for radiotherapy. It was also a great group where we all connected, and it really helped me.

Scary C is lonely until you find the right group of individuals who you can connect with, and you are there for one another regardless of diagnosis.

From my experience with Scary C, I had amazing people around me, but I was still lonely until I accessed various support groups, like Macmillan, Helen Rosalind foundation, online Macmillan group connected with different individuals sharing their different experiences. On the forum it didn't matter what your diagnosis was or what stage you were at, the ladies shared freely without holding back just to help one another. Helen Rosalind Foundation was just like my second home, we connected well, talked about everything our fears, pain, every question was answered and encouraging words were said. I began to live again, my drive and why to live became stronger, my faith was reignited.

I am really looking forward to giving back to my community, by setting up a foundation where women going through Scary C can access support from diagnosis to after treatment regaining their confidence back. It's great to connect and find the right support.

CHAPTER TEN

How did I ever get here?

I t was a lovely year 2016. In the UK everyone was looking forward to summer. And like most people, I love summertime. According to the Cambridge dictionary, Summer is the season of the year between spring and autumn when the weather is warmest, lasting from June to September. In this time of the year, days become warm, hot, and long, while nights in this season are the shortest. The sun shines so bright, and everything around is whispering to go outdoors. There are plenty of leaves on the trees, more bright and beautiful flowers and trees and plants producing fruits.

Summertime is also that time, most people plan to travel outside London or travel abroad. I normally don't travel out in the season because I feel we are being exploited with huge fares because they

81

know most people or families are really looking forward to it. I will normally plan different outings in the UK with my family as quality time with my family is very important. Guess what!! This summer was different; I had concluded plans to travel to Nigeria. It was my younger sister's wedding, and I was going to attend, I didn't care if the transport fare was high or not. In fact, I wasn't travelling alone but with my siblings; we were all going for this special wedding.

Prior to the wedding day, my church NCC Edmonton also had their yearly plan for 'family month' and 'outstanding weekend' and various other events planned. I was looking forward with earnest expectation to all these events especially the 'Outstanding weekend' but the unusual happened, yes, the unusual and unexpected happened.

On this very beautiful Saturday, I woke up looking forward to the planned event in Church with high expectations which promised to be a fun day also. I went into the bathroom and while washing myself I felt something hard, small like a pebble on my breast, I thought to myself that this was a bit strange and unusual, it was certainly never there. I felt it again and kept poking at it... I wondered what this was. But I left for the church anyways.

The event was great and outstanding as usual, I was very absorbed in it that I didn't give a thought to what I felt earlier not till when I went to bed and felt it again, I was a bit confused and puzzled... no crazy thoughts yet. I decided to keep an eye on it and being a woman of faith,

82

I prayed over it without any bother. As the days rolled by, I observed that it was bigger and bulging out. I became concerned, booked an appointment with my GP, and continued praying this time intensely that whatever this is, should disappear.

While waiting for my appointment date, I decided to talk to my mentor DR Femi Idowu of blessed memory who was a doctor by profession and a doctor of the word of God. He was the resident pastor in New Covenant church (NCC) Edmonton at the time, he prayed with me, advised me to keep my appointment and update him on the outcome. As my appointment date drew nearer and nearer, the lump grew bigger and bigger, I became uncomfortable but continued to reassure myself with God's word.

My GP was very helpful, she examined me and made a referral instantly, she wasn't saying much but there was a lump and action needed to be taken. I was booked for a mammogram. This was the beginning of the ordeal; I was hanging in there and praying and Dr Femi Idowu was also praying with me. The much-awaited day finally arrived, and I went for my mammogram with trepidation. I had never had one before, this was my first time ever hence, I wasn't sure of what to expect, to be honest I was terrified but was just trusting in God to strengthen and uphold me.

At the Breast clinic I met a couple of ladies I knew way back, we got into different conversations, which was relaxing for me, but they came for routine checks not been referred like me though. I kept my poise and waited. Finally, it was my turn. Oh, my world, it was a very painful process; I remember screaming uncontrollably from the pain. The radiographer was very supportive, but no one could help me. I knew something was wrong, I had to wait to have a biopsy which was equally painful.

The breast consultant spoke to me reassuringly, explained the process to me but also told me not to come alone when coming back for my result. Was that a hint or what?

Then the wait for the result. Yes, wait. I was told by the consultant that the result will be ready in a few weeks, and I will be invited back to see her, and we will take it from there. Then it felt like the longest wait of my life, I tried not to think about it, my hubby tried reassuring me that there was nothing to be worried about and doctor Femi kept reminding me of God's promises for my life, he would counsel me at the end of Sunday service. It all strengthened me and finally I received my appointment letter from the breast clinic to see the breast consultant.

It was time to find out if the lump discovered was malignant or benign. When the cells in the tumor are normal, it is benign. Something just went wrong; they overgrew and produced a lump. Malignant in simple words is when the cells are abnormal and can grow abnormally and uncontrollably, they are Cancerous cells, and the tumor is Malignant.

I held on to my faith, believing that all will work well for my good. I can't honestly say I was hundred percent confident, but I was positive and hoped for the best. This time around I wasn't going alone to the hospital, my adopted big sister offered to come along with me, it was a great day to catch up again and we prayed before setting out for my appointment.

What was it going to be? It was a busy day at the breast clinic and the doctors were half an hour behind schedule. It was going to be a long wait, I kept myself occupied browsing through all the magazines I could lay my hands on. After a couple of hours waiting, I noticed three of the nurses all in blue uniform going inside the consultant's office, but they didn't come out and I heard my name called from that same office... Yes, this was it. This was the dreaded moment.

I went in with my sister right behind me and we weren't alone, we had company. The three ladies in the blue uniform were there with a welcoming smile on their faces and the consultant asked us to take our seat, introduced the ladies as the breast team and said they were going to be present throughout the meeting. I wasn't sure why I needed them there but decided to focus on what the consultant had to say as she opened my medical file. She confirmed my date of birth and went on to the size of the lump and unto the result of the mammogram and biopsy, finally the awaited result...

The breast consultant put the file down and looked straight into my eyes and said, "Olufunke, I am so sorry it's not good news." You know the rest guys...I would like to stress that it is very important to check our

SURVIVING THE SCARY C | Olufunke Ogunmodede

breasts regularly as ladies and be conversant with our breasts so as to be able to know what is normal or abnormal, what they look and feel like. For me it looked and felt wrong, something wasn't right. Whatever was bulging out was never there before, definitely an intruder. It wasn't normal. Early detection is key! This view has wide currency.

Mandy Gonzalez born August 22, 1978, is an American actress and singer, best known for her leading roles in Broadway working on CBS drama. Mandy said breast Cancer tends to impact Latina women at a younger age than the general population. "I was very fortunate that they were able to catch it early." It's very important for women to know that early detection is key. She first had a screening which revealed a cyst and was asked to come back in six months, she had a nagging feeling and returned for an ultrasound that led to the discovery of a tumor behind the cyst which a biopsy revealed was Cancerous.

Mandy said, "research has given me a second chance."

Research has come a long way now giving people a second chance and lives are being saved. Early detection and timely treatment increase the chances of survival. The objective of the (WHO) new global breast Cancer initiative is to reduce global breast Cancer mortality by 2.5% per year, averting an estimated 2-5million deaths. Through this initiative WHO is working in unison with other United Nations (UN) agencies and partner organisations in providing guidance to governments on how to strengthen systems for diagnosing and treating breast Cancer. Groups to address health promotions, early detection, timely breast Cancer diagnoses, comprehensive treatment, and supportive care.

Early detection and early treatment are very important in the Scary C journey. If detected early, be grateful, if late, it does not matter be grateful for life and fight the fight. We are survivors.

CHAPTER ELEVEN

If you are ever going through any emotional trauma; stay positive. -
Olufunke Ogunmodede

My mentor of blessed memory once said that whatsoever situation we find ourselves, whatever we may be going through, God has already made provisions for us. This is very true, right from diagnosis to the end of treatment and even now, whatever the need there is a provision for it. This provision comes in different forms like resources, amazing people around you that want to help you with things, hold your hand, speak encouraging words that are uplifting to you and honestly all this makes a huge difference to someone going through the Scary C journey. Going through Scary C helps you to appreciate little things we often take for granted; hugs, smiles and a listening ear goes a very long way, hugs communicate reassuring messages; stay strong, thinking of you.

Scary C is a very overwhelming ailment that you must stay positive despite the odds. It was the lowest point of my life, but I believe God held my hand all through. God knows the highs and the lows of my life right from the beginning and he has made provisions for it all.

If you have just been diagnosed, in between treatment or living with this ailment, please do not give up. Don't quit. I know that there are days where you just want to scream… enough no more. I totally get it, the amount of blood they take from you consistently, the needles piercing your skin… just a scratch they often say, finding a vein and not finding it, emotional and physical fatigue, appointments at the hospital. It's crazy but during all these you must put the fight on, be positive. There is no easy way to say it, you really must fight the fight but it's not over until it's over. We might feel broken now but look on the bright side, we are not and cannot be defeated by Scary C.

Every survivor has their unique Scary C story, your story is different from mine, but our common ground is to pick ourselves up and fight this life changing disease. We will not be defined by Scary C. We are fearfully and wonderfully made, we are beautiful. As a survivor I know we are rendered powerless with so many things happening on this scary journey. What do I mean? There are things like losing my eyebrow hair completely; my sore toes and fingernails, losing the entire nail initially disempowered me, my thoughts were all over the place, but I took control of my thoughts to stay positive. How you deal with these changes really matters. I concluded that I am not defined by all these challenges or changes happening to my body, there is more to me and my entire life. I am beautiful!

As discussed previously in chapter four, I cannot but over emphasize the importance of staying positive during trauma. I encourage you beautiful ladies reading this book or going through the Scary C journey to take control of your thoughts because when you do, every other thing begins to align. There is so much power within our very own thoughts. Let's focus more on our mind and thoughts, while others are focusing on the impact and the treatment.

My beautiful ladies, in concluding this chapter I would also like you to pause for a second and think about that loved one who is constantly there taking care of you, shift your gaze from yourself completely, your challenges and focus on them and ask yourself one question… how are they really feeling?

They are scared, miserable, frightened, tired, some don't know what to say anymore but keep going and hoping for the best, not giving up on you, attending the appointments with you, holding your hand through difficult and painful moments. They are very hopeful and if they are hopeful to see you get better, you cannot QUIT on them.

SURVIVING THE SCARY C | Olufunke Ogunmodede

I have had the opportunity to speak with survivors and ladies going through treatment, sharing their pain and experiences in support groups and online community and it's been encouraging to see the fight they are putting in not quitting and this in turn is helping others who are extremely scared and overwhelmed, to have a different outlook to (Scary C) IT IS NOT A DEATH SENTENCE.

I love this quote...

" The times we count as dark or low, every often gives us the opportunity to say with confidence to someone in the future...." I have been there; hear me you are going to be fine. - Wandetrains

Yes, Beautiful you are going to be FINE!!

91

Valuable lessons from Scary C journey.

The journey was indeed tough but there were also valuable lessons I learnt during the journey that will surely stay with me forever. I have outlined them below and hope that you will find them useful.

Families and loved ones are very important in one's life and they are not to be taken for granted. They are happy to see you happy and ready to share the burden if you let them. No matter the level of crises I am faced with, I will take a step backwards and think positively of overcoming the situation, blocking out fear. Trusting God completely is simply releasing yourself without thinking of how God will do it. Simply believe you are healed according to God's word. Accept help when offered, you can't do everything. Remember every little help counts.

We tend to bottle things inside and pretend to be strong outwards, but I learnt to let it out by crying when I had to cry or just talking about what I was going through with a loved one. Listening to my body and taking a break. Perhaps, this is one of the most important nuggets! I would say 'Have a Me time' even now. Please don't wait until you are ill.

What you consume daily is very important. What are you eating that is harmful to your body? It is always good to take an audit and cut down on the 'Nice to have'. To connect and relate to others goes a long way, it's priceless!!! It makes a huge difference.

Planning financially has its own reward. To be well educated about the right insurance and benefits available to us. This is one of the most important – you do not want to worry about your finances as well as your health. Take appropriate steps and put measures in place. Employment benefits are very important. What benefits are you entitled to at your workplace? Think about it and please read the company's policy and ensure that you are absolutely clear.

A TRIBUTE TO MY MENTOR

This book cannot be concluded without paying tribute to doctor as I usually call him. Late Rev Oluwafemi Bosun Idowu (FBI), was a doctor by profession and a doctor of the word of God. He was the associate pastor in the New Covenant Church Edmonton from 2006 to 2018 when he was commissioned to Pastor the Stevenage Branch (New Covenant Church, Strong Nation).

I found out that when you are too familiar with people, you don't really give it a name or label but casting my mind back on my relationship with Doc, he was my Mentor.

Hey Doc, I wish you were around to witness the launch of this book and hold it physically, I believe you will be super-duper proud of me. I was looking forward to surprise you with my half-written book after the lockdown restrictions were lifted, little did I know it wouldn't happen. You breathed your last and went to be with your maker on the 21ˢᵗ of July 2021.

Doc, you were always my go to person, if I ever had any nagging questions on different aspects of life. Whether it was my job or spiritual and personal life. A couple of times I called you from work for guidance in dealing with some situations and people.

In short, I trusted in your wisdom. You were such an encourager, right from the start of the Scary C ordeal, you stood by me, praying with me, lifting my spirit, sharing, and backing every word with God's word, the scriptures brought light. I can remember after service you would sit next to me to share a word of encouragement with me. You were a man of few words but with a great sense of humor. I remember vividly, you coming to see me after my surgery, I was on a Zimmer frame, I couldn't stand upright but the first thing you said to me was, 'Funky, you had a free tummy tuck on the NHS'…very funny Doc. No matter how intense or challenging the situation, you would always bring out the fun aspect which might not seem funny to me at all at that very moment but later when I look or think back, I will surely see the humor and crack up.

You were a teacher of the word. You dissected the word and taught it brilliantly. 'Mind Gym' was your baby, this was a platform where you encouraged us to take a daily pill, you referred to the word of God as a daily pill that needs to be taken to empower and increase our faith. It was a platform where you broke down the word of God for people of different ages to understand and relate to God's word in a very simple way.

It was something to always look forward to. 'Healing Academy' was another initiative of yours where you taught on Spiritual healing using the scriptures in the Bible, another avenue to empower people and increase their faith. This was the avenue where I learnt that no matter the challenges we ever face in life, we should believe that God has

95

made provisions for us, and this really ministered to me through the Scary C journey. Doc, you taught me how to read my bible in context which I will forever be grateful for, going through the sessions at the Healing Academy, you would ask me several questions putting me on the spot but all you did was to give me a full picture and understanding of God's word. There are a couple of books in the bible that are not easy to understand, but you break it down effortlessly, debunking all myths. You loved God no doubt about it.

You were such a good listener but a man of few words with a wink or grin that says it all; don't worry it's well, God is faithful. You stood by my sister when I did not have the strength to! You had a name for everyone and always with a grin. You were kind to a fault, always going out of your way to put a smile on everyone's face.

Doc, what can I say? You had the heart that cared completely, and you had the grin that brought so much pleasure.

You fought the Scary C battle, you prayed to the end, your faith didn't waiver for a bit right from the beginning to the end. No wonder, your final words to your loving wife were, "I am at peace. I am peaceful." You won.

Doc, heaven is a beautiful place because they've got you. A saint has been received to Glory. Angels are celebrating.

Your life was one of kindly deeds, a helping hand for others' needs, sincere and true in heart and minds, beautiful memories left behind.

96

Goodbyes are often hard to say, they hurt so very much.
Though you're not gone. You still remain in the minds, hearts,
and lives you've touched. – Angela Williams

Goodnight, Doc. You are forever missed.

Final words:

Hey, my beautiful ladies. I have spoken about my faith and my gratitude to God. If you are wondering who this God of mine is and you would like to know him, or you might simply be saying please pray with me for healing.

It will be my honour to lead you to Jesus, the king of kings, the Lord of Lords, and the great healer...

Take a moment to bow your head and simply say this prayer: "Lord Jesus, come into my life and be my Lord and personal Saviour. Please forgive me all my sins, cleanse and sanctify me, make me pure and whole again. Thank you for loving me.

Thank you for dying on the cross for me. Thank you for the price You paid for me with the blood you shed. I receive you as my Lord and Saviour. I accept your love and forgiveness. Help me to live completely for you from this moment.

Thank you very much. Amen."

Believe that you have been forgiven and made whole. Now, you have a brand-new life, you can go ahead and enjoy all the benefits of salvation. By His stripes you are healed, personalise it and make it your daily confession.

Remember it's not over until it's over. We are beautiful and God is in control. We cannot and will not be defined by Scary C.

If you would like to know more, you could connect with the author via the following platforms:

Instagram: https://www.instagram.com/funkieiamceo
Facebook: https://www.facebook.com/olufunke.ogunmodede
Mailbox: funkie50babe@yahoo.co.uk

Yours faithfully,

Olufunke Ogunmodede.

Printed in Great Britain
by Amazon

21623206R00058